kvell

A Word You Should Know

Barbara Edelston Peterson

Post Hill Press

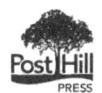

A POST HILL PRESS BOOK
ISBN: 979-8-88845-936-2
ISBN (eBook): 979-8-88845-937-9

kvell:
A Word You Should Know
© 2025 by Barbara Edelston Peterson
All Rights Reserved

Cover design by Jim Villaflores

This book, as well as any other Post Hill Press publications, may be purchased in bulk quantities at a special discounted rate. Contact orders@posthillpress.com for more information.

This is a work of nonfiction. All people, locations, events, and situations are portrayed to the best of the author's memory.

Although every effort has been made to ensure that the personal and professional advice present within this book is useful and appropriate, the author and publisher do not assume and hereby disclaim any liability to any person, business, or organization choosing to employ the guidance offered in this book.

No part of this book may be reproduced, stored in a retrieval system, or transmitted by any means without the written permission of the author and publisher.

Post Hill Press
New York • Nashville
posthillpress.com

Published in the United States of America
1 2 3 4 5 6 7 8 9 10

To Nana Lee

*Your kvelling instilled in me the confidence
to believe in myself, and appreciate
my personal spirit that made me a curious
and happy person. I still hear your
sweet words of encouragement.*

TABLE OF CONTENTS

Introduction 9
Foreword 13

CHAPTER ONE: **the power of kvell** 19
CHAPTER TWO: **what is kvell?** 25
CHAPTER THREE: **how to kvell** 39
CHAPTER FOUR: **the benefits of kvell** 53
CHAPTER FIVE: **the science of kvell** 69
CHAPTER SIX: **kvell at home** 77
CHAPTER SEVEN: **kvell in the workplace** 83
CHAPTER EIGHT: **kvell with strangers** 89
CHAPTER NINE: **kvell as a habit** 97

Acknowledgments 103
About the Author 107

INTRODUCTION

THROUGHOUT THIS BOOK, I CELEBRATE both the traditional and modern interpretations of kvell.

"Kvell" is traditionally understood within Jewish culture as a feeling of immense joy, happiness, and pride, typically experienced by parents or grandparents over their children's or grandchildren's achievements. This sensation is best described as an internal bubbling-over-with-joy, occurring within the home or at a school, sport, or social event.

Growing up in a Jewish household where kvelling was standard practice, I learned it well while also reaping the indelible benefits from my parents' and grandparents' constant encouragement, reinforcement, and pride. This nurturing environment helped me to thrive. I discuss all of this in more detail in Chapters One and Two.

As a caring young girl, teenager, graduate student, and eventually a wife and mother of two daughters, I kvelled in many non-traditional settings with noticeably positive impacts. And even though my applications of kvell weren't within the traditional context, the effects of gushing over, complimenting, loving, and encouraging others brought too much joy and mutual benefit to ignore. This led to my dream of sharing the lessons from this vibrant practice with the rest of the world, and to someday write this book.

FOREWORD

FOREWORD

IT'S NOT EVERY DAY YOU meet a person like Barbara. In fact, it might not even be once in a lifetime. I've been blessed to meet, and befriend, someone who is unequivocally the Queen of Kvell.

When you hear Barbara's voice, there's a tone of warmth and excitement. When you ask her opinion, you can feel how she engages you with her whole being. Her heart is open. She is genuine and loving. Most people don't know how to do what Barb does naturally. She unabashedly embodies the concept of kvell.

She doesn't apologize for feeling deeply and she doesn't hold back. At the end of one of our first phone meetings, she said, "Shifrah, I just love you." She meant it, and I could feel the essence of kvelling—it uplifted me.

Barbara has cultivated kvell into her being. She embodies it fully. She kvells over people, places, and things. Over everything. You see it in her eyes—she celebrates and honors goodness! She honors herself by kvelling over her own and her daughters' achievements. It's not ego. Rather, it's a genuine sense of pride and happiness that shines through to her beautiful smile.

As you read this book, you will get to know Barb's unique perspective, one she wants to share with the world.

Barbara's intention is for you to adapt kvell into your own life. Take every opportunity to pump people up. Help them believe they are doing well, or on the way to something very good.

Learn the lessons of this book well, apply them, and watch your life and the lives of others blossom. The power of kvell is extraordinary, almost intoxicating.

—Shifrah DeWitt, Jerusalem

CHAPTER ONE

the power of kvell

KVELL SHAPED ME TO BE who I am today. It shaped me to be a bold, ambitious, adventurous woman at sixty-eight years old.

I was born to a Jewish family in White Plains, New York. While my family was not perfect, one thing my parents excelled at was kvelling over their three daughters. To my parents, particularly my father, we were the smartest, most talented, and most capable girls to have ever been born. Each of us daughters agrees our father made us feel inordinately special. We could see and feel his excitement bubbling up inside, but it didn't stop there. He let us know how proud he was of our actions. He was kvelling!

It wasn't that we were spoiled by all the encouragement. It was more that our parents were our biggest fans. Our dad was more demonstrative; he had a way of grinning, letting out a high-pitched whistle, and waving his hands—sometimes doing all three at once—that told us we were going to hit the mark and then some.

It wasn't that we could do no wrong either. Our dad was direct in letting us know about mistakes. He was as critical of us as he was proud, which in itself illustrates the positive power of kvell. Because of our dad and mom's kvelling, we learned from a very young age that we could—and would—accomplish anything.

My sisters and I have taken dramatically different paths through life, but what has stayed within each of us is the feeling that there are no limits to who we can become or the heights we can reach. I thank the kvell in our house—it buoyed us.

I know that kvell is what motivated me from childhood into adulthood to live by extremely high standards and to believe that I could achieve almost anything I set out to do. It most likely had everything to do with my becoming a world champion in the demanding sport of off-road triathlon, becoming a published author back in the 1990s, and earning two master's degrees: one in psychology and one in Eastern philosophy.

A generation later, it's quite possible that my daughters' lives were also shaped by the power of kvell. As grown women, they are ambitious, accomplished, and caring people. I venture to say the kvelling over my children plays a significant role in their confidence, ongoing achievements, and positive relationship with life. How could it not?

I came to see that kvell is a love language for children, adults, and the whole world. It's such a simple way to communicate with a beautiful effect. It's spontaneous, genuine, and freeing—all through a touch on the shoulder, a wink of the eye, a smile bubbling into a cheer, or a compliment. It has enough power to move the world in valuable ways.

Kvelling encourages self-belief, leads to initiative, and brings out human capability, from one person to another. If every person on the planet kvelled just once per day, think of the impact that 8.1 billion people could have using the most positive universal language.

That's the whole point! Kvell is potent. It taps into potential, transforms hope into reality, okay into yes, and complacency into action. Kvelling between family, friends, and even strangers energizes abilities that might otherwise lie dormant. It's a powerful practice giving life to the human spirit. It's a word everyone should know. Start kvelling and watch what happens.

> Kvelling encourages self-belief, leads to initiative, and brings out human capability, from one person to another. If every person on the planet kvelled just once per day, think of the impact that 8.1 billion people could have using the most positive universal language.

CHAPTER TWO

what is kvell?

HAVE YOU EVER HAD SOMEONE say something so clear and affirming to you, or encourage you in a noticeable but nonverbal way, that it changed the outlook of your whole day, or maybe your whole week, or even your life? That person might have been a family member, a friend, a teacher, a teammate or coach, a boss, or even a stranger. What they said, or did, stayed with you. It lifted your spirits and made you look at yourself a little differently. It made you feel understood and empowered, that you were on the right track. They were kvelling over you!

Derived from the Yiddish word *kveln*, which means "to be delighted," "kvell" also has roots in the Middle High German word *quellen*, which means "to well, gush, or swell," according to *Merriam-Webster*. In Yiddish, the special language of European Ashkenazi Jews, kvell is "seen yet not heard"—it happens internally as a "bubbling over" of pride and excitement over the *kinder* (children). In my family and other Jewish families as well, kvell evolved from an internal experience into an external show of approval, excitement, and exuberance—sending a loud and clear message that you are adored, you are recognized, and you are doing, or did, a good job.

You may know a variety of Yiddish words that have been assimilated into the English language, such as: "schlep," "schmooze," "klutz," "schmuck," "chutzpah," "schmutz," "mensch." There's also "kvetch," which is the exact opposite of kvell. And of course, "oy vey" or "oy vey iz mir," expressing dismay or exasperation. I hear people use these words all the time, both Jewish and non-Jewish people.

I have to stop and kvetch here. The problem with the above words that have become common expressions in the English language is that many of these words have negative connotations. To be fair, the word "mensch" is a well-known Yiddish word and it's positive. It refers to a person who has a strong sense of self, someone whom you would want as a trusted friend, colleague, or life partner. Yet it's almost always reserved to describe a male. The real complaint however, is that among all the common Yiddish words that are used regularly, there is one Yiddish word missing, that few people outside of Judaism know. That word is "kvell."

Kvell is expressed as a surge of positive emotion from one person to another. It relays admiration, belief, marvel, excitement, and celebration over someone's effort to achieve and the achievement itself. Kvelling between family, friends, colleagues, or strangers raises the ante on what's possible. When someone kvells over me, watch out, world! It gives me the feeling I can do anything without a sense of limits. Kvelling has an instantaneous effect that translates into courage, confidence, acceptance, gratitude, and finally, "Yes, I'm good (enough), and I actually *can* do this!"

So then, why "kvell"—a vibrant Yiddish word and concept—hasn't been assimilated into the English language is beyond me. We need it! We need every available positive word to offset the negative ones. We need to bring the power of positivity into our conversations, our actions, our lives, and into the lives of others all over the world. I am writing this book to introduce kvell—the word as a noun and verb—because it should play a special role in our lives. It's long overdue that a bright light shines on the word "kvell," and that it be introduced, understood, and expressed by everyone. Kvelling brings out the best in people, with mighty potential to make the world a better place.

The Dictionary of Jewish Words defines "kvell" as "to burst with pride, particularly at the accomplishments and achievements of one's children." The Jewish-English Lexicon, a website created by Professor Sarah Benor, author of *Becoming Frum: How Newcomers Learn the Language and Culture of Orthodox Judaism*, defines "kvell" as to "feel or express pride, to be extraordinarily pleased." And Chabad.org says that "kvell" is a verb and "its Yiddish iteration implies the glow that comes from the success of the people you care about." When I shared my dream to write this book with a handful of rabbis and Jewish friends, explaining the power of kvell is too valuable to ignore, they kvelled over me! Yet in truth, not everyone appreciated this iteration of kvell, and so I apologize for the upset this might cause. Kvell is an ancient practice. Kvell is also a celebration of people's greatness. And there's a lot of greatness to kvell over!

Kvell is an especially genuine, vibrant communication. It's a spontaneous and personal expression of joy, approval, and admiration. There's not a speck of negativity, jealousy, or envy in kvelling—rather, it's the exact opposite. And

> Kvell is an especially genuine, vibrant communication. It's a spontaneous and personal expression of joy, approval, and admiration.

there's no way to prevent someone from the spontaneity of kvelling! There's only room for happiness, affection, and appreciation for a family member or another fellow human being. What's inherent in kvell is the innate understanding that there is no limited amount of it; it will never run out. Just like there is no limited amount of abundance or love on this planet. Plenty for everyone, all of the time. We just have to do it, share it, express it. That's the spirit of kvell.

Think for a moment back to your childhood. Envision a time when you did something and a nearby adult exclaimed, "Awesome job!" Maybe you drew a pretty picture, learned to write in cursive, climbed a tree to help a neighbor rescue their cat, volunteered to clean away debris after a storm, or found the courage to swim across a lake for the first time. Or maybe you wrote your own collection of poetry, or helped serve lunch at a food bank, or spent the day passing out pamphlets in support of a good cause. Did your grandparent, parent, neighbor, or another adult cheer about it? Did they give you a big hug or pat you on the back? How did their enthusiasm and awe of your achievement make you feel?

If you're anything like me, you glowed from the inside out because that adult loved it, marveled at it, and cheered for you. You felt a sense of accomplishment and pride. You owned the fact that you did well. That is the power of kvell.

Earlier, I said the opposite of kvell is kvetch. If you are unfamiliar with this Yiddish word, it means "to complain." When we complain or criticize, we are as far as we can get from kvelling. Think again of those good feelings when you received praise and felt special. I imagine you felt light, happy, and a bit like you could conquer anything.

Now just for a split second, remember a time when you felt ashamed or dismissed in childhood or as an adult. Maybe your dad had a bad day and snapped at you for being too loud when he came home. Or maybe a glass slipped from your hand and shattered, and your brother called you clumsy, a klutz, or stupid. How did that make you feel? When something like this happened to me, I felt reduced to a tiny, gloomy creature. My spirits were crushed. I felt darkness and sadness creep into my veins. These are antithetical to kvell experiences, and not the space we want to inhabit.

I have a story to share. It was a late evening in September 2012, the night after I had signed a publishing contract for the second edition of a book I wrote about surviving bed rest, and the night before I was to fly to Europe to compete in two big races. In fact, my bike box and bags were packed and waiting in the hallway for the 3:45 a.m. airport shuttle. Just before bedtime, I realized

I needed one more thing for the trip: a cap that would be the perfect gift for the race director. So, I climbed to the very highest shelf in our open closet to find the cycling cap. Just as I reached into a box and pulled it out, my foot slipped, I lost my balance, and I dropped fifteen feet to the carpet below. I let out a piercing scream, my husband and daughter came running, and we all looked down at my feet, which immediately turned purple and changed in look from two human feet to two irregular bags filled with tiny pebbles. Unfortunately, that's what happens with bilateral heel fractures. The trip to Europe just got canceled.

I spent four months in a wheelchair. I swam every day with fracture boots on, and after the swim I would slip into a dry pair of fracture boots. Finally it was my very first day back to the pool without the wheelchair. I had just progressed to crutches and still had to wear the two bulky fracture boots. I still had to get to the locker room by elevator, where I was now joined by an older woman. I knew her as one of the oldest swimmers with a remarkably nasty disposition. I'd never seen her smile; rather, she seemed to disapprove of most everything and everyone. Suddenly I realized, being together in the elevator, there was something I enjoyed about her. She was full of fight and she was tough. I could see it in her eyes and I liked it. She recognized me and moved towards me, getting close to my face. My bending over the crutches made our heights equal. With a shocking half smile, she said, "Look at you! You're doing great!"

I was truly caught off guard by her now very loud voice, and the kvelling. She moved in closer—my ears and face became red. I couldn't figure out why she would think that I, with my wet hair, dripping swimsuit, and fracture boots, looked great. I responded with, "Gee, thanks for the encouragement. You're a nice woman."

Just then the elevator began to move. She backed away just slightly and blurted, "No, I'm not. I'm not a nice person at all."

I was speechless, trying to figure out how to respond.

She moved in closer again, and with barely a breath between words, said, "I am not a nice person at all, but I have a soft spot for you. Do you want to know why I feel for you and why I carry you in my heart?"

I was frozen, and not because my wet swimsuit, hair, and boots were now icy. I wondered, "Oh God, what next?"

The woman continued, "When you were in dire straits, looking so fragile in the wheelchair and obviously in pain, you came out of the elevator one cold, dark morning on your way to swim. You had huge plastic bags on your legs over those terrible-looking black casts. You looked entirely overwhelmed. We were both at the front desk waiting to get questions answered. You complimented me on my sweater. It wasn't even seven a.m. and you were so weakened by your severe injury but eager to live, and I was ready to cause a problem and complain like I always do. And because of you, I stopped myself."

The elevator doors started to open but the woman wasn't done. She said, "I marvel at you. I tell everyone about you—that you kvelled over me!—and you know something, you have changed me. Because of your kindness and your positivity even at the lowest possible point anyone could be, you still had kindness in your heart. And plenty of energy, and you gave it to me! You showed me another way to be, a better way. And I'm almost eighty."

The elevator landed, the doors opened, and the women's locker room beckoned. But neither of us moved, other than me putting my hand into the doorway to keep the doors from closing again. It was clear to me she wasn't finished, so I smiled. She sighed and stopped talking. I looked into her eyes and asked her name.

She said, "My name is Sarah, and I know who you are, Barbara, my friend."

To this day, she's calmer and kinder, and our interactions are always pleasant. All because I chose to kvell in response to her habit to kvetch.

CHAPTER THREE

how to kvell

IN CASE YOU'RE UNSURE ABOUT how to kvell, and wondering if it involves words, physical gestures, or external emotion, the answer is it's any and all of this. It's a genuinely positive and excited response that is directed at someone. Kvelling always translates as a deliberate expression of encouragement, reinforcement, affection, admiration, excitement, and congratulations. I'll spell it out for you here.

KVELL: A TO Z

- Admire, Adore, Applaud, Appreciate
- Believe, Bless
- Cheer, Congratulate, Commend, Compliment
- Delighted, Delivery
- Exuberant, Extol, Elevate, Elated, Euphoric, Enraptured
- Fired up
- Glorify, Glee, Glow
- Hail, Honor, Happy
- Infatuated
- Joyous
- Kindness
- Love
- Marvel

- Nice
- Overflowing, Openhearted
- Praise, Pride, Passion
- Quiver
- Reinforce, Reassure, Rejoice
- Strong interest and feelings, Squeeze, Shaky with excitement
- Thrilled
- Up
- Very happy, Victorious
- Waving, warmth
- Xtravagant, Xcellent, Xaltation
- Yes!
- Zest, Zeal

Traditionally, kvell expressed exaltation, happiness, pride, and love between Jewish elders and children. I grew up being kvelled over by two elderly grandmothers and my parents. One could deduce that I was "trained" to rejoice in others. In fact, that is exactly what I do inside and outside my family. I kvell over my two daughters, their friends, my friends, our teachers, coaches, and strangers. I kvell over achievements involving special focus and effort. I kvell over people I don't know, who look as if they are trying their best to accomplish something, often outside of their comfort zone, and to watch this is deeply exciting—so much so that I kvell over it! I kvell over someone trying hard to achieve something for the first time. I kvell over people who are achieving great feats, over and over: champions, celebrities, influencers. I kvell over the car wash guy who does a conscientious job, and my UPS driver who always has a smile on her face and leaves treats for our dog at the front door. I kvell over all garbage and recycling truck drivers who take their jobs to heart. In these different cases, I kvell through verbal compliments expressing gratitude and joy, or waving my hands and showing a thumbs-up, probably close to how my dad kvelled.

Kvelling inside the family, or at work, or other places outside in the world, comes in all shapes and sizes. It doesn't have to be verbal or involve physical contact. Several years ago, I witnessed how a teacher's nonverbal kvelling moved an antagonistic situation with a student to a calm, happy, and positively meaningful situation. Ms. Steiner, a high school AP Chemistry teacher, took extreme issue with my daughter, Foreste, and her rigorous ski racing schedule. Unexpected successes kept her away from school for six weeks. Although this teacher and student agreed to a plan to keep up with homework assignments as well as labs, after two weeks Ms. Steiner demanded Foreste drop out of the class. With a sense of urgency, Foreste communicated from Sugarloaf Mountain in Maine to Berkeley High School in California, insisting they stick to the agreement. After all, each assignment had been turned in, and labs had been completed at other schools. Six weeks to the day, on the first day back to class, Foreste walked nervously into the classroom. Her teacher took a good look, apparently raised her eyebrows, and without a word walked over to Foreste with an unusually large smile, where she extended a warm pat on the back and gestured she go to the front of the classroom to be the first to share the final report. In seconds,

Foreste knew she was being congratulated and actually celebrated—without an exchange of words. As it turns out, Ms. Steiner stated so all could hear, "Well done, Foreste." The final grade in AP Chemistry was an A, and the final result was a student brimming with self-confidence and maturity. Ms. Steiner's nonverbal "welcome back" was a powerful kvell, full of recognition, appreciation, and validation.

Once, I watched an ocean lifeguard walk the beach to alert everyone there were bees hovering on the sand. He suggested we keep an eye out and pass it along to others. I promptly followed him back to his chair to kvell over him. I kvelled over his going the extra mile in his job. I let him know that witnessing him take time and energy to care about people on "his" beach was inspiring, and that his level of kindness and conscientiousness would serve him in all future jobs and relationships. I let him know he served as a role model, showing total strangers how to care about others, and how to do their job earnestly. His face was one big smile. He thanked me and just kept smiling!

I simply cannot hold back when I see someone striving to hit the mark, do good, take pride in a job, and progress in their lives. When I notice someone or something superb, I am compelled to kvell. Sometimes I applaud, shout out "Bravo," or flash a big bright smile. Happy eyes speak volumes!

If I go to a new vegan restaurant, my favorite local pizzeria, a hair stylist, a small local bookstore, or a retail clothing shop that demonstrates excellence, I call them afterwards, or write a note or send an email saying, "Wow! Well done! Loved the experience! Thank you!" And when I discover a product or read a book that's absolutely terrific, I tell everyone I know, "Hey, check this out—it's not to be missed!" Often, I am told how my encouragement energized them, spurred them on, activated the capable person hiding within, and elicited the bold and courageous personality that had never come out before, ready to shine outwardly in the world.

That's kvelling! And I am a huge believer that our world needs more of it!

Kvelling through writing is less common than kvelling through face-to-face communication. I'm a big fan of both, and I kvell a lot through emails or notes. I sent this email to a manager at the Madewell store about one of her employees:

> Dear Lauren,
>
> I met Victoria at the Fourth Street/Berkeley Madewell, and thanks to her...Madewell has become one of my favorite places to shop!
>
> I simply cannot tell you how fantastic she is, although you probably already know this. She is an earnest individual who operates with 100% intention for excellence. She is especially friendly and knowledgeable, yet unimposing. The store and your customers are lucky she's there.
>
> Thank you for hiring terrific people who care about their job and the customers' shopping experience ~
>
> Barbara

We never know how our written kvelling will affect someone or what it will mean to them, not just in the instance they receive it but later on in their lives. A friend, Catrin, shared a letter she received when she was in France in 1977. She's held onto it all of these years because of its kind words and kvelling:

Hello Catrin, how are you? I hope you're as strong and active as I remember you at your best, that's the way I think of you. I don't think my memory of you has been distorted by time. I remember you as an uncommonly good force, and also someone with a particularly unusual quality of energy; more persistently creative, personally and externally by your own facility to use your life, your existence as a tool to carve enjoyment from the world in the best way. Catrin, that sort of thing rubs off onto people, it's a beautiful thing to have, never stop.

My love to you,
Thomas

Kvelling can also be done without using words. My friend Kim mentioned a teacher's kvelling and encouragement that was mostly nonverbal. She shared with me, "If he hadn't kvelled over me, with a warm smile and nod of the head, I may have lost my way. His ability to see that I had talent allowed me to see it too! At age fifty-four, I still remember that encouraging pat on the back and that he called me 'A good egg.'"

More than eight billion people call Earth home. There are endless ways to celebrate the good in human beings! And when this happens, it truly helps make the world a better place for everyone.

Sadly, too many people spend too much of their time kvetching. Too many people—from all cultures and demographics—whine and complain. It not only raises their blood pressure to dangerous levels, but it reduces the positive ripple effect. Please: either step up and fix what isn't working or seek out a positive alternative. Then enjoy it, and kvell over it!

In summary, everyone kvells differently, but what's always the same is the positive, affirmative, reinforcing message that is delivered.

> *...everyone kvells differently, but what's always the same is the positive, affirmative, reinforcing message that is delivered.*

CHAPTER FOUR

the benefits of kvell

THE BENEFITS OF KVELL lie in the spontaneous burst of affection, the open show of interest, the excitement of celebrating someone's capability and potential, and the good feelings from good energy. The benefits from such delight are innumerable, but in a word, kvelling elevates life for both the person kvelling and the recipient.

You might ask, "Is it really that big of a deal? What difference does an impromptu dose of encouragement or a dash of attention really make?" The answer is: it only takes a single second, a single act, and a single person to make a difference in someone's life, whether they're in need of reinforcement, hope, or healing. The global effect, compounded, is exponential.

Chapters One and Two covered a few of the benefits of being the recipient of kvelling, including that it boosts self-esteem and advances one's perspective of what's possible. To really understand the benefits to both the giver and receiver, it's necessary to understand a few basic aspects of life.

Regardless of when, where, and how you entered into this world, life is an everyday endurance test. It's a mountain that every human climbs. It's a journey over terrain that's forever changing. In truth, the going can be tough, and there isn't anyone who wouldn't welcome certain things to aid with the journey: water, food, rest, deep breathing, and support from others.

For the recipient, kvelling supplies the confidence, hope, belief, respect, momentum, happiness, appreciation, and more that help us navigate ways to live our best lives.

I'll explain this for you in detail:

CONFIDENCE

Confidence is the feeling that you can rely on yourself, that you can trust your own ability, or that you can count on someone or something else. For example, if someone tells you you can do something repeatedly and expresses enthusiasm over each step you take to get towards your goal, you will start to believe you can reach the goal.

> You might ask, "Is it really that big of a deal? What difference does an impromptu dose of encouragement or a dash of attention really make?" The answer is: it only takes a single second, a single act, and a single person to make a difference in someone's life, whether they're in need of reinforcement, hope, or healing. The global effect, compounded, is exponential.

Some of that self-assurance is inborn, but most often, self-assurance grows with each success, and blossoms with kvelling. The impact of kvelling—whether over you or me, a world leader, a top athlete, a celebrity, an influencer, or anyone else—fortifies courage and conviction to go forth and achieve. In my life, it was my father who kvelled over me, and the result is that I deeply believe in myself, in my actions, thoughts, expectations, and goals. I am secure enough to attempt most anything, and that in itself feels empowering. Kvelling is very potent.

Think for a moment about a toddler learning to walk; even imagine yourself taking your first steps. The enthusiasm of the people around us, the clapping and cheering that propelled the next steps, instilled in us the belief that we could do it, again and again. That was kvelling, and it's what created confidence bubbling from within you, and the certainty of "Yes, I can walk."

HOPE

Hope is an optimistic state of mind that is based on the expectation of a good outcome in one's life. There's power in the knowledge that someone believes in you. Kvelling increases hope, one kvell at a time.

An example of this occurred to me one day when I was at the pool. I noticed a young boy who was doing a swim workout while he was on vacation. His dad was at the end of the pool with a stopwatch. I got the feeling the swimmer wanted to break through to a faster time. The dad was kindly doing his son the favor of being a timer and recording his splits. I got excited by watching this strong swimmer muscling through the workout. I decided to see what would happen if I cheered him on for his next set. I talked to his father and found out he was training for an upcoming championship meet. I asked the son and dad if I could cheer—I hoped it would make him faster.

Right away, I could see a difference. My attention (affection) was enough to bring out a little smile at the wall with more drive and energy to perform.

Off he went, flying through the water. I was cheering loudly, so he could hear me through the water. "Go! Go! Go! You've got this!"

His dad and I watched as his speed increased and he sliced through the water differently than he had on his previous laps. He swam more self-assuredly. He gave a lot. He nailed his personal record.

The swimmer looked up at me, totally out of breath this time with a big smile. "Thanks. I'm not sure what happened, but that made a huge difference."

My kvelling and the loud, happy cheering gave him hope that he could best his personal record. I wish I could see where this moment might have taken him since.

Kvelling has the power to uplift a person to greater heights than one can imagine. It's often others sharing the belief in our ability that transfers to our own self-belief and confidence. Kvelling is a special link to hope and possibility.

BELIEF

Belief is tied to confidence and faith that you can tackle anything. Few people have the belief that they can do this; most often they let their fears or "reason" talk them out of even trying. It takes some dreaming, passion and desire, setting goals, and receiving encouragement from others (being kvelled over) to accomplish certain tasks.

I went to Tibet to mountain bike across the Himalayas, including up to the base camp of Mt. Everest, and onward into Nepal. Just before it was time to go, I lost confidence in my ability to do it. In the throes of altitude sickness and intense fear about what lay before me, I fell into despair, feeling as low as I've ever experienced. Serendipitously, while sitting listlessly in the lobby of a hotel in Lhasa, my phone rang. It was my daughters, there before me on FaceTime. It was miraculous to see them, the very last day of acclimatizing. Immediately into the conversation, my voice cracked as I shared my reluctance to begin due to feeling low stamina, zero strength, and big fear. They started to kvell: "Mom, you're so strong, you've done so much to prepare, and we already know you'll love it once you start!"

My youngest daughter raised her voice: "Mom! You'll never know until you try!"

And my older daughter chimed in, "Yes! Trust yourself, just go for it, and we'll be cheering for you every day. We are with you!"

The rest is history; their kvelling fortified the start and stayed with me for the entire adventure. Upon my arrival to Everest Base Camp, I dedicated what I felt was a supreme personal triumph to them and to the power of kvell.

MOMENTUM

In high school science class, we all learn Newton's first law of motion, that an object at rest stays at rest and an object in motion stays in motion (unless acted on by a force). Humans can follow this pattern too, and kvelling provides the "force" to get people moving and improving.

At my hardest moments while competing, I use self-kvelling to propel myself forward. I repeat over and over: "Yes I can." It fills my head and whole body with hope, down into my cells. It delivers fresh strength, and a happy mindset. It's a new and positive momentum. Should the momentum shift, and I start to feel that I can't go further, I intensify the kvelling by silently repeating these words over and over: "I am strong" or "I am good" or "I love this." The result? An upsurge of focus, energy, hope, and the belief that I will finish strong.

The benefits of kvelling are that it produces momentum on the cellular, cerebral, and spiritual levels. And when we feel momentum on all three levels, we are unstoppable and can accomplish our heart's desires.

RESPECT

We feel respect when we believe we are taken seriously, that we are trusted, and that we have good judgment. Kvelling celebrates a person's accomplishments and triumphs. Kvelling cheers the person on to even greater things. And it does so without offering any advice or admonishment, so respect is inherently conveyed in the process.

APPRECIATION

We flourish inside and outside when we are valued and validated, when someone communicates their appreciation of who we are, what we are trying to do, or what we have achieved. A kvell could be a shake of the hand, pinch of a cheek, wink of the eye, or pat on the back. Whatever form it takes, it affectionately expresses appreciation. It says, "You matter. You are seen and heard. You are fantastic!" And who doesn't want to feel special?

The hope, belief, momentum, respect, and appreciation—all the parts of kvelling that uplift the recipient—have just as positive an impact on the kveller. The act of kvelling offers the kveller many benefits, including happiness, connectivity, more robust health, increased awareness and empathy, likeability and more love, and more positivity. It allows them to leave an imprint on others.

HAPPINESS

The feelings of excitement, celebration, compassion, and reinforcement that build within just seconds combine into the welling up that defines kvell. What is expressed in two words, a nod of the head, a happy waving of the arms, or a loud cheer originates as an exuberant, happy, and inspired inner experience for the kveller. What triumphantly uplifts the person being kvelled over has already uplifted the person delivering the kvell.

Being enthusiastic about what someone else is doing or has accomplished makes us feel more lively, animated, and happy. Kvelling sets off a reaction in the brain and releases endorphins that make us feel good… for a moment, for a day, or for the rest of our lives. The power of kvelling is so much greater than it just being a nice thing to do. It's beneficial neurologically, mentally, and socially.

CONNECTIVITY

Sometimes we think about life in terms of our home, our possessions, our work, our family, our education—the big stuff. But life is really made up of little moments, the times when we kvell and are kvelled over and never forget the momentous energy that moved us to a better place in life.

MORE ROBUST HEALTH

Expressing kindness and care to others—as opposed to staying closed off and to yourself—provides a boost to our psychological, emotional, and physical health. Several studies tell us that the simple act of helping others flushes out negative feelings like anger and aggression, reduces our own stress levels, alleviates depression, and boosts our immune systems. Kvelling is a form of help and health. Additionally, with all the loneliness and isolation in today's society, you never know what a kind word can do to turn someone's life around.

INCREASED AWARENESS AND EMPATHY

Kvelling reflects an increased awareness of what others are attempting to accomplish or are doing; it opens our feelings for all people, of all ages, where we are not only aligned with their triumphs but also their struggles to attain their goals. Empathy is not a static trait though. We are born with it and practice it from the moment we smile as infants. We can increase our empathy and awareness intentionally in a number of ways: by listening and talking to others frequently and by providing compassionate kvelling. In 1975, Ed Tronick did the famous "still face" experiment. His findings serve as a profound understanding in developmental psychology and show how strong our need for connection is. Specifically, this experiment told us what happens when connection does not occur:

"Tronick described a phenomenon in which an infant, after three minutes of 'interaction' with a non-responsive expressionless mother, rapidly sobers and grows wary. He makes repeated attempts to get the interaction into its usual reciprocal pattern. When these attempts fail, the infant withdraws [and] orients his face and body away from his mother with a withdrawn, hopeless facial expression."

LIKEABILITY AND MORE LOVE

For the love of kvellers! Who doesn't want to be around someone who is positive, who offers kind, encouraging words, and who lifts others up? The fact is, we tend to attract people into our circles who act like and have interests like we do. When we focus on the positive energy within us and the positive things that are empowering others, we create goodwill and feelings of gratitude and goodness that reverberate around us. This makes us likable...and maybe even more lovable.

Kvelling isn't just a way to deposit love into the outside world; it is always a way to deposit more love inside yourself. For we, too, like ourselves more when we are contributing and making the world a better place.

LEAVING AN IMPRINT ON OTHERS

Kvelling is a way of leaving your mark on the world without knowing the final outcome. Think back to the story earlier in this chapter regarding the swimmer reaching for a new personal record. I helped him achieve that by kvelling over him, but I will never know the final impact my kvelling had.

POSITIVITY

This energy is infectious!

For example, consider the practice of "paying it forward." Kvelling is like paying it forward as it encourages others to follow your kvelling lead and to encourage and celebrate the people in their lives. This chain reaction can look like many different situations: When a person feels positivity from an interaction with another, that is kvell. When someone admires your approach to a task and lets you know, that is kvell. When someone gives you a compliment, or stands up on another's behalf, that is kvell. When you feel pride in yourself from another's kvell, that, too, is kvell.

These are the social benefits of kvelling. The person kvelling is empowered while empowering someone. It is a ripple that starts within and emanates outward. When we receive a message that positively affects our self-esteem, our self-confidence, our happiness, and our ability to perform, it is a powerful force.

So, yes, the benefits of kvelling are exponential on both a personal and social level.

Author and motivational speaker Leo Buscaglia wrote about kvelling (although he didn't call it "kvelling"): "Too often we underestimate the power of a touch, a smile, a kind word, and listening ear, an honest compliment, or the smallest act of caring, all of which have the potential to turn a life around."

I hope you will embrace the many benefits of kvelling, for both the giver and the receiver, and find ways to touch another person's life by kvelling over them today. When we open our eyes and hearts, we'll find that the opportunities are endless.

I invite you to stop here for a moment and reflect on some of the most impactful words you have received from others. Words that helped you keep going when you wanted to quit, pushed you further than you thought you could go, or inspired you to live out your dream.

CHAPTER FIVE

the science of kvell

YOU MAY THINK THAT KVELLING is a bit of fluff, part of positive psychology and feel-good vibes. But kvelling has a scientific basis and a body of research that extols the power of kvell. A study published in the journal *Social Cognitive and Affective Neuroscience* used functional magnetic resonance imaging (or MRI) to view how affirmation and self-affirmation activates the reward centers in the brain. These reward centers are what "light up" when you experience anything pleasurable, such as eating your favorite foods, winning a prize, or receiving accolades for a job well done.

University of Pennsylvania Professor Christopher N. Cascio, principal of the study, said, "Affirmation takes advantage of our reward circuits, which can be quite powerful." The same study showed that hearing encouragement or affirmations can also restore self-competence. This is similar to what's stated in the book *Words Can Change Your Brain*, written by Andrew Newberg, MD, and Mark Robert Waldman. They claim "a single word has the power to influence the expression of genes that regulate physical and emotional stress."

In summary, positive words strengthen areas in the frontal lobes and promote the brain's cognitive functions. They activate the motivational centers of the brain into action and build resiliency. Conversely, a single negative word or kvetching activates the amygdala or fear center. According to Newberg and Waldman, the right words can transform our realities. They write, "As our research has shown, the longer you concentrate on positive words, the more you begin to affect other areas of the brain. Functions in the parietal lobe start to change, which changes your perception of yourself and the people you interact with."

All of those positive words (whether you are the giver of them or the receiver or both) can help boost your immune system, decrease your stress levels, and give you joy and purpose. It certainly helped me on a particular day in my life, related in the story that follows.

It was a long steep hill on my bike, and I was struggling in the middle of it, on a very hot summer day. Just as I sat back down from climbing out of my saddle, digging deep into the pedals, another cyclist whooshed past. He couldn't see that it was getting to me, but it was. Just as he got close, he shouted, "Get it, girl! You're amazing!" That was exactly what I needed: a kvell coming from a fellow cyclist! That kvell in that brief moment gave me new life. Immediately, my energy shot up. My excitement about the ride exploded, and my appreciation for the recognition, for him believing in me, powered me to the top of the hill with a very full heart.

Newberg and Waldman also wrote that our facial expressions have the power to inspire trust in others, and that body language can "convey more meaning than words can ever capture." So, remember that the next time you kvell. May your beaming facial expressions, your nodding and encouragement, be just what a person needs to fire their endorphins, make them feel good, and stimulate their brain's reward areas so that they believe in themselves and excel in their tasks and lives.

A few kind words, excited eyes, and a smile coming from someone else's heart can push you up every steep hill. Kvell *is* the elevated energy to make it to the top of any mountain, that day and all days. Kvell acknowledges another person's output: their energy, effort, talent, intelligence, and fortitude. When we kvell, it's like shooting positive arrows into the individual, *and* into the world.

And don't think kvell is good for only people. Have you ever had a pet? Gushing over the accomplishments of a dog or a cat causes the animal to show more affection, want to please the person more often, and repeat the behavior for which they are being praised.

Plants also respond well to kvell, confirming that old adage that it is good to talk to your plants. But be careful what you say. One study had students talk positively and kvell over a plant for thirty days. That plant thrived and grew and seemed "happy." To a separate plant, the students talked negatively and used bullying and kvetching language. By the end of thirty days, that poor plant was withered and near death. The researchers noted the study showed the power of our words, even on life incapable of expressing emotion.

CHAPTER SIX

kvell at home

KVELLING AT HOME IS THE ancient love language of Jewish people, mostly associated with grandparents and parents adoring their children. It's a cultural practice filled with warmth and happiness that has filled the hearts and souls of young and old for multiple generations. Kvelling then and now epitomizes celebration and joy. And gratitude. Its richness also has value outside the home, to be shared with neighbors, colleagues, playmates, teammates, and others. Today, our world is calling—even begging—for kvelling, inside and outside the home.

Kvelling cancels kvetching. Kvelling cancels cruelty. Kvelling elevates everyone.

My father was a great kveller, as I mentioned earlier. My mom did her fair share too. One of my fondest childhood memories is bringing home my favorite big book of poetry after library day, and having my father read selections to me. After his readings, I'd make up my own poems and share them out loud with him. Oh, how I loved building sweet little poems, and he truly loved hearing my creations. He clapped enthusiastically after each of my poems, hugged both me and my big book of poems, and

> Kvelling cancels kvetching.
> Kvelling cancels cruelty.
> Kvelling elevates everyone.

repeatedly encouraged me to keep creating poetry. This type of kvelling was rich in love, heritage, affection, and true belief...in me. And I believe it is why I love to write today. Especially poems.

When it came to sports, my father's enthusiasm for all three of his daughters was off-the-charts kvelling! Since he had no sons, he taught us to play football and ice hockey, and run track-and-field hurdles. He wanted us to be "good" and let us know we were his superstars! We learned proper technique for each sport, how to snap the football to the quarterback, and run like hell for a touchdown or hockey goal. His zealous kvelling carried over not only to our love of sports but also to our confidence in successfully tackling most of life's hurdles.

My mom's kvelling was different from my dad's, but there was plenty of it. One example that was typical of my mother occurred when I was twelve years old, while on a fun family vacation. At the time, I was a fairly serious springboard diver and while we were away, there was an important competition that couldn't be missed—the pre-qualifier for the state diving championships. Since we were all enjoying ourselves so much, I asked if we could skip the big drive and stay put. Immediately, my mother began to kvell, "Oh no, no, we're not missing this! Our wonderful diver who has extra special talent needs to shine at that meet, and I bet we'll have a winner sitting next to me on the car drive back." We went, I qualified, and I won states later that year.

Now, as a mom of my own two daughters, I'm a huge kveller, and I think by now we all understand where it comes from! My daughters are also kvellers…they kvell over their friends and each other! An example of this is when Foreste (the ski-racer daughter in the chemistry class) earned her spot at a World Cup ski race, her big sister, Hilary, upon hearing the news, immediately purchased plane tickets to be there in support of her sister. While in the stands as a spectator, on the coldest, snowiest day of that winter, Hilary was filmed by a local TV station. We were told by the reporter she was the "most expressive" spectator. Of course, she was kvelling over her sister!

When there's kvelling in a household between family members, the benefits include:

- Happier children
- More optimistic and intrinsically motivated family members
- Increased self-confidence
- Cooperative relationships: less jealousy, more sharing
- Better mental health and well-being
- Greater social competency

CHAPTER SEVEN
kvell in the workplace

CHAPTER SEVEN

Scoring in the workplace

THE POWER OF KVELL CAN benefit *every* kind of work environment, whether in schools, offices, remote work, or geographically dispersed workforces. Studies have shown that reinforcement and encouragement that happens in the workplace can determine your level of job satisfaction.

Daniel Goleman, author of *Social Intelligence: The New Science of Human Relationships*, explains that the cumulation and frequency of positive versus negative moments not only determines our satisfaction but also our abilities to perform. Goleman writes, "Small exchanges—a compliment on work well done, a word of support after a setback—add up to how we feel on the job."

Kvelling as a type of positive encouragement isn't warm and fuzzy fluff. It's a compelling tool to elevate people of all ages, including colleagues. One of my friends, Roman, told me a story about one of his first jobs as an engineer. His office was a room with no windows; it was a space to house a chair, desk, computer, and him. He was given the task of creating a salvage study of a six-hundred-mile-long natural gas pipeline despite his lack of knowledge about or experience with natural gas or pipelines. The job was isolating, which made him feel disconnected from the company, removed from his coworkers, and discouraged. But he did the work he was asked to do and produced the required report.

A couple of weeks later, in a meeting with all of the managers, the vice president, who was not known for praising employees, began kvelling over the report: "This is an example of excellent performance, and a job well done." The kvelling boosted Roman's mood, made him feel more positive about himself and his employer, and gave him greater confidence for future tasks. It eventually got him promoted to management. Had that kvelling not happened, Roman might not have had a successful career at that company nor the ones that followed.

Studies have shown that employees who are cut down tend to shut down, and ones who are kvelled over for their accomplishments go on to do even bigger and better things. This may be because of the dynamics of many working environments. Goleman writes:

> "For many working people, coworkers become something like a 'family,' a group in which members feel a strong emotional attachment for one another. This makes them especially loyal to each other as a team. The stronger the emotional bonds among workers, the more motivated, productive, and satisfied with their work they are. Our sense of engagement and satisfaction at work results in large part from the hundreds and hundreds of daily interactions we have while there, whether with a supervisor, colleagues, or customers."

Aaron Barnes, CEO of BRM Institute (Business Relationship Management Institute), writes in an article titled "Language Matters" that positive language (such as kvelling) helps elevate business communication, promotes collaboration, breeds innovation, and drives value. This is because an encouraging atmosphere gives people more courage to express themselves, to be creative, and to do their best work.

Kvelling in the workplace can transcend time zones, country borders, pay grade, and job titles. Anyone can kvell over anyone else and help change the course of workplace interactions and culture.

Kvelling in the workplace can appear magically, such as at an annual evaluation or inside a written quarterly review. When there's kvelling, there's power, an upward pull, and next-level expectations. In general, all employees, including managers, directors, and executives, love to feel appreciated, seen, and heard in support of their belief they are contributing to something bigger than their often seemingly mundane roles. Kvelling helps connect people further inside the company and it helps set people apart when it bestows the kudos they have earned. In an age where workforces are geographically dispersed and much of our communication is electronic, creating feelings of connection is more important than ever.

CHAPTER EIGHT

kvell with strangers

WHEN YOU KVELL OVER STRANGERS, you may not know them very well, but you can relate to their experience or accomplishments, and you feel proud of them. Much of the kvelling I've shared as examples is "distanced" kvelling: a boy at the pool I didn't know, a guy passing me on my bike, and an older woman in the elevator while I was recovering from bilateral heel fractures.

One of my favorite kvell stories—with a stranger—happened in the cosmetic department of Nordstrom. A young person in the process of transitioning into a woman stood alone behind the makeup counter, wearing tons of makeup. Evidently, it was a new beginning, a safe place to experience a whole new identity.

As a sensitive person, I wondered for a moment what this individual must have been going through. I admired the kind of courage and conviction this process involved, on many levels. My emotions welled up inside; I had already started kvelling, but quietly. I was proud of this person. I wanted to let them know I was on their side, that if I had directly verbalized my thoughts, I would have said, "Right on!"

I looked this person in the eye and said, "You look beautiful."

We both smiled and looked soulfully at each other. Then I asked them about my lipstick color.

On one hand, I knew it wasn't my business to kvell. But on the other hand, I was bubbling over with joy seeing someone discover their authentic self. My warm eyes and smile spoke volumes—I was kvelling. And I could see the joy within and without being received. I felt comfortable enough to ask, "Do you leave the store with your beautiful eyes…or do you change when you go back home?"

Somewhat timidly and with a couple nods of the head, they said, "I wash everything off before I go home."

I chose the right color lipstick, I bought it, and we chatted some more. Leaving the store, I was warmed by our compelling encounter. But kvelling has a lasting effect.

One week later, I received a box from the department store. A gift box was filled to the brim with an amazing assortment of samples including Jo Malone perfume, Prada creams, and small Chanel lip glosses. While sifting through the goods, I found a handwritten note that read:

Dear Barbara,

It was a great pleasure to meet you and help you at the counter. I really appreciated your kindness and interest in me.

You made my day, actually you made my whole week. You made me feel like I was good, that who I am mattered, and that I would be o.k. in this world if I trusted being me.

What an amazing feeling to have made a difference in someone's life, to have made someone's life a little brighter.

M

The magic of kvell is the electrical charge that happens when someone conveys their belief in your action and greater possibility. It's the feeling of "Yes I can."

The power of kvell is awe-inspiring. Because something *stunning* happens energetically when we feel surges of empowerment throughout our whole being. So much more possibility and life happens when people are encouraged.

I wrote this book to say yes to the questions "Is it possible to help each other attain greatness just by saying an encouraging word? Could kvelling actually change an outcome?" And, ABSOLUTELY!

Negativity is toxic and exhausting. Kvelling is the opposite; it's empowering, uplifting, healing, and energizing.

A friend kvelled over a cashier at her local grocery store when she told me the story of how she witnesses the clerk kvelling over "her" shoppers: "You've never seen anything like it! This tiny Hispanic woman *kvells* over every customer who comes through her line, celebrating who they are by remembering their names, their dogs' names, and celebrating certain details she's learned about their lives. When the cashier is finished checking the items, she says something positive to each person. The customers adore her positive energy and her kvelling so much that they line up for her register even when other lanes are empty. People go out of their way to experience her kvelling." This is a perfect example of the power of kvell—how great it makes people feel when they are kvelled over and how once you are known as a kveller, people will seek you out to brighten their days.

> *The power of kvell is awe-inspiring. Because something stunning happens energetically when we feel surges of empowerment throughout our whole being. So much more possibility and life happens when people are encouraged.*

Within kvelling over strangers is the concept of tribal kvelling, which means you are taking pride in and making positive comments over someone in your own tribe or minority group. For example, as a fellow Jewish woman, I kvelled over Ruth Bader Ginsburg and took pride every time she gave a speech, wrote a brief, or walked into the Supreme Court. We tend to kvell over the accomplishments of those in the groups to which we feel akin.

When you kvell over a stranger, you may never know if your kvelling makes any difference in their life. But knowing the impact is only a part of the point. I kvell because someone or something makes me very excited. I also know it increases good vibrations on the whole planet. I join with Maya Angelou, who said, "I've learned that people will forget what you said, people will forget what you did, but people will never forget how you made them feel."

CHAPTER NINE

kvell as a habit

WHILE KVELLING WORKS BEST WHEN it is spontaneous and filled with passion, starting any new mindset or action requires awareness and intention. Let's compare it to starting a better eating program or deciding to exercise. We can talk all we want about how we want more positivity and health in our lives, but unless we actually take steps to make things a reality, all of our wishing will be just that: a hope and a dream.

Kvelling is the same way. If you aren't already in the space where you compliment people on their accomplishments or encourage them regularly to succeed, but you want to, you will need to consciously make the effort. Science tells us it takes at least twenty-one days to adopt a new pattern or to create a habit that will pour forth from you automatically. So, if you commit to twenty-one days of reminding yourself daily to find someone to kvell over, you will find the habit of kvelling much easier to sustain.

As with all habits, we find it most sustainable if we start simple or small and then build from there. You wouldn't decide to run a marathon and on day one run 26.2 miles. First, you'd put on running shoes and do a combination of running and walking for a mile at most, especially if you've never run regularly. And then each day, you might add a little distance, or a hill, or some other challenge—what is officially called the compound effect. Studies show that after the initial days, if you compound the habit by just 1 percent each day, you will improve more than 37 percent in a month. And each day your muscles will get stronger, and your lungs will develop more capacity, and you'll develop stamina. But each of these things would take time and practice.

For kvelling, starting simply or "small" might include a goal of kvelling over one person per day every day for a week. And then during week two, kvelling over two people per day could be the intention. It is human nature by week two of creating a new habit that we may want to slack off and forget the commitment we've made to ourselves. In order to combat this, I'd suggest placing a few Post-it Notes in bright colors on your bathroom mirror, on your refrigerator door, and wherever else you look a lot. Write things like "Kvell over someone" and "If you like it or love it, kvell over it!"

ACKNOWLEDGMENTS

TO MY DAUGHTERS, HILARY AND FORESTE—watching the way you navigate through such productive lives, fills me with the greatest joy and pride and keeps me kvelling.

To Dennis Baker, Lynne Rabinoff, Anthony Ziccardi, Melody Stanford Martin, China Jones, Quinn Delaney, Mimi Doll, Diane Hollman, Heidi Winslow, Gail Kvistad, Marion Burch, and Carol Johnston—thank you for sharing your encouragements, and constructive criticism throughout this journey.

Lastly, my deepest appreciation goes to an anonymous friend for their countless reviews, discerning questions, brilliant critique, and overall help enriching the final product.

ABOUT THE AUTHOR

BARBARA EDELSTON PETERSON holds dual master's degrees in clinical psychology and eastern philosophy. She is the author of six books, including *The Bed Rest Survival Guide* (1998), *In My World* (2023), *A Whole Person Makes the Whole World Better* (2023), and *A Whole Athlete Makes the Whole World Better* (2023). Barbara is a motivational speaker and sports psychologist, leading international workshops and seminars. In 2016, she founded the Whole Champion Foundation, a nonprofit dedicated to personal, social, and environmental responsibility.

She lives in Santa Barbara, California, and is the mother of two grown daughters.